sounds like this

First steps in phonics, linking sounds with letter shapes

Katie Kitching

Line drawings by Katie Kitching

First Published in 1993 by
BELAIR PUBLICATIONS LIMITED
P.O. Box 12, Twickenham, England, TW1 2QL

© 1993 Katie Kitching
Series Editor Robyn Gordon
Designed by Richard Souper
Photography by Kelvin Freeman
Typesetting by Belair
Printed in Hong Kong through World Print Ltd
ISBN 0 947882 26 X

D1299529

Acknowledgements

The Author and Publishers would like to thank the staff and children of Buckland Infants School, Chessington, Kingston-upon-Thames, for their contributions and help during the preparation of this book. In particular, they would like to thank Deborah Mistry, Jeannine Byrne, Amanda Rose and Claire Dorey for their help with the artwork; and Ann Bristowe, Frances James and Ann Kerr for their helpful suggestions.

They would also like to thank Lucy Allen (5) and Kate Hindley (7) for the cover artwork.

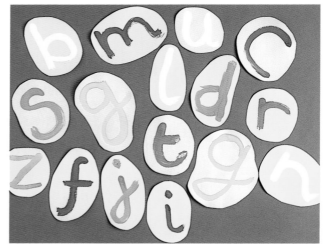

NOTE:
1. It is realised that writing styles vary from one school area to another, and you may wish to change the style used throughout this book.
2. Copyright: Permission is granted to photocopy the worksheets for classroom use only.
3. The worksheets should be enlarged to A4 size for classroom use.

Contents

Use letter shapes in creative activities:
- Traced in sand
- Painted using various techniques (see border for 'C')
- Made from dough, clay or Plasticine

Introduction

If children are to become competent readers - reading for meaning, information and enjoyment - we must adopt many strategies to help them along the way. One of these strategies is making the links between the visual representation of individual letters and letter strings and their sounds: developing children's phonological skills and making analogies with print.

Before introducing written letters it is essential to make sure that children are aware of the sounds which make up language. It is not always obvious to a child that sounds which we hear can be translated into print on a page. Listening skills should be developed, refining the pupils' auditory discrimination and enhancing their awareness of rhyme and alliteration. Ability to discern sounds is vital to later reading success, and activities should be devised to highlight and emphasise the sound which is heard.

The teaching of phonics should not be seen in isolation, but as one important aspect of the teaching of reading, to be used alongside other cueing systems. It will enhance the child's awareness of print, and accelerate reading progress - and although it should not be over-emphasised, phonics are a vital aid in decoding print, and essential for reading success.

In this book, ideas are given for teaching the most common sound of each of the twenty-six letters of the alphabet. There has been no attempt to develop this further into a 'phonics programme'.

The suggested activities can and should be used with pre-readers as an oral activity, reinforcing the heard sound. Younger children should enjoy the activity, talking about what they are doing, with the adult emphasising the target sound. Make sure children can hear clearly - often it is necessary for them to see lip and facial movements as they practise the sound with an adult.

Many of the ideas can be used with older children who, for one reason or another, have not connected sounds and letter shapes. It is not intended that all the activities should be attempted, but it is useful to have a wide range to draw on for children who have difficulty in remembering and using phonological information. It is often possible to combine learning a sound or sounds with other areas of the curriculum. The creative material for this book was collected during a reception year - the displays for *u, k, w* and *e* were all part of a topic on Weather.

Katie Kitching

Classroom ideas

A display table incorporating the sound currently being targeted (in this case 'd')

- It is important to choose examples of words that include the target sound in its purest form, and not part of a blend which requires further analysis to identify the new phonemes (for example, use 'tap' rather than 'trap').

- Try not to give consonants a following vowel sound, e.g. 'h' should be breathed rather than emphasised ('huh'). Always make sure the children can hear clearly and are pronouncing the sound correctly. Insistence on a quiet classroom is essential to achieve this.

- Writing letter shapes should be linked with letter name and sound. It is valuable to have an adult to direct letter formation so that the letter sound can be emphasised and correct formation supervised at the same time. Well-briefed parent helpers are of great help here.

Carpet tiles are an excellent substitute for felt boards - Velcro adheres very well to the surface

CHILDREN'S NAMES

A natural starting point when encouraging an awareness of spoken sound is the child's own name. Each child could have his/her own motif which begins with the same letter as the name, e.g. Katie - key; Dominic - dog. The motif should appear wherever the name appears, on class lists, name card, peg name, registration card (a set of name cards with a small piece of Velcro on the reverse side, which children transfer to a felt board on arrival in school). Talk about the children's special pictures - 'Why has Alistair got an apple on his name card?' 'David - duck, d..d..' 'Can you think of something else Mikaela could have had on her name card?'

Names could be slotted into named pockets, matching name to name.

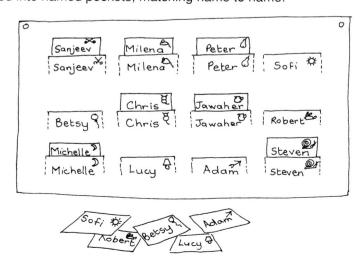

PICTURE CARDS

It is useful to have sets of picture cards which illustrate the heard sound for class and group activities. A duplicated set enables them to be used for pairs games, matching table with table, sun with sun etc. The cards can be sorted into sets, depending on the initial letter sounds - apple, anorak, ambulance, arrow etc. Throughout the book there are pictures for each sound which can either be copied or photocopied, coloured and made into cards.

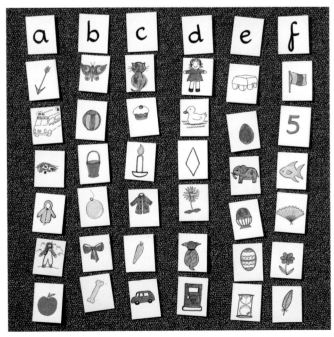

Smaller versions of the cards can be used in a felt-board game, where the child sorts into sets according to initial letter sound.

ALPHABET CARDS

Sets of cards using pictures and the letter shape whose sound begins the object in the picture is an obvious extension to the picture cards. One or two sets could have lower case letters on one side, capitals on the reverse. Again, use these for games and general language work. Allow children free access to the cards - they may devise their own games, extending and developing their awareness of sounds and letter shapes. Use the picture and alphabet cards in general classroom routines, for example, when giving out drinks or lining up - 'If your name begins with 'b', you may......' Later the cards can be used when children are tackling emergent writing.

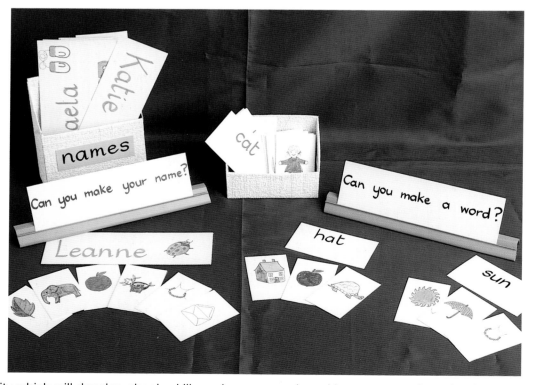

An activity which will develop phonic skills and awareness is making names and words with the picture cards.

ZIG-ZAG BOOKS

Zig-zag books for each letter of the alphabet are an interesting way of introducing letter shape and sound - the children could make their own versions.

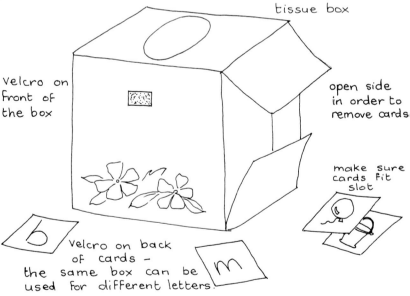

Two boxes are needed - children sort cards according to initial sound of picture name.

tissue box

Velcro on front of the box

open side in order to remove cards

make sure cards fit slot

Velcro on back of cards - the same box can be used for different letters.

POSTING GAME

Small children enjoy posting games. A simple game can be quickly made using two empty tissue boxes. A small strip of Velcro enables letters to be changed. Use letter shapes which are quite different to begin with - 'j' and 'u' for example. Later, choose letter shapes which are similar, for example 'b' and 'd'.

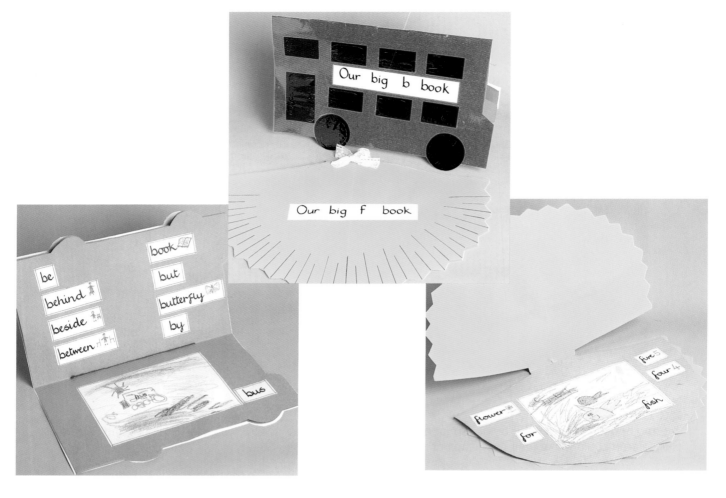

BIG BOOKS

Planning and making large class books is an activity which can involve all the children. Shaped books give extra interest.

Some ideas for each letter of the alphabet are as follows: apple, bus, cat, door, egg, fan, gate, house, ink, jug, kite, ladybird, mushroom, nest, orange, panda, quilt, rabbit, sun, television, umbrella, vase, wall, box, yoghurt pot, zebra crossing.

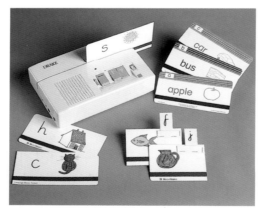

LANGUAGE MASTER

Language Master games are an excellent addition to classroom resources. This is a system where the child is presented with the printed letter and the sound on the same card, which is fed through the Language Master recorder. Children can do this themselves, giving them the opportunity to practise phonic skills independently.

It can be used in conjunction with earphones which cut out classroom noise, and which also override the built-in speaker. A set of alphabet cards is available from Drake Educational (see Reference section) and teachers can make their own sets using blank cards.

SORTING GAME

A game which will stimulate language and encourage phonic awareness is the draw-string bag game. The children sit in a large circle, around two plastic circles which are marked with a letter in the centre. A draw-string bag of objects is passed round - each child removes an object and places it in the appropriate circle. In this case, objects whose name begins with 'b' or 'd' were chosen.

BIG PICTURES

These can be used to develop observational skills and to encourage children to scan and look for particular items. A set of cards directing children to look for objects will add to the value of the activity. A piece of wrapping paper has been used in the above example.

BOARD GAMES

Games which could be played with parent helpers are a useful addition to classroom equipment - the most effective are those which teachers devise with specific aims in mind. Here are two examples:

Game for four players

A die with a letter on each face
24 small cards - 4 for each letter
Each player has a base card with
  six pictures

Talk about the pictures on each child's card before commencing the game. Children take turns to throw die - they find the picture on their card which begins with the letter sound they have thrown, then select the correct small card to place on the picture. If the picture is already covered, the play passes to the next child. The winner is the first to have all pictures covered.

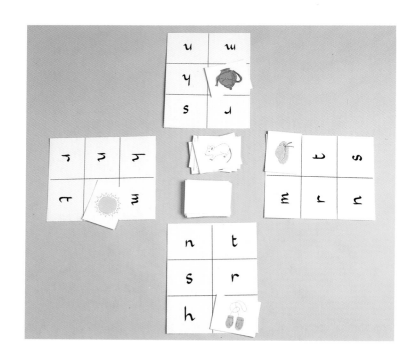

Game for four players

Four base cards, one for each player
Each card has six letters in six boxes
Set of 24 small cards
- four pictures for 'm' (mouse, mushroom, monkey, mittens)
- four pictures for 'h' (house, hat, holly, heart)
- four pictures for 'r' (rocket, ring, rocking horse, roof)
- four pictures for 'n' (nest, necklace, net, nail)
- four pictures for 't' (tent, tortoise, table, teapot)
- four pictures for 's' (sock, snail, scissors, sun)

Before playing the game, go through the pictures, talking about the sound at the beginning of each. Place the cards in a pile, upside-down, in centre. Children take turns to take the top card. They use it to cover a letter, or miss a turn if the letter is already covered. In this case, they put the card to the bottom of the pile. The winner is the first to have all letters covered.

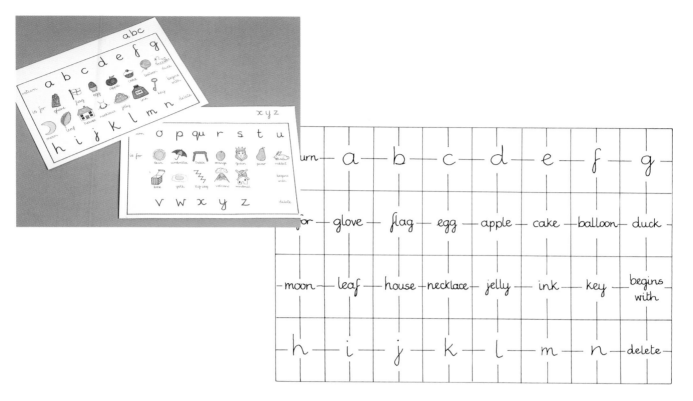

COMPUTER GAMES

There are computer games which reinforce phonic knowledge in particular. Teachers can devise their own programmes, using a concept keyboard. These have the disadvantage that only words (not pictures) can be displayed on the screen, but they are a valuable reinforcing activity as children become more confident. Print-outs can be used to make individual sound books. (A photocopier could be used to enlarge and darken the print-out.)

TAPE RECORDER ACTIVITIES

A story could be found for each sound in the alphabet. (Some have been suggested in the Reference section, on page 69.) These could be recorded on individual tapes for children to use with earphones. It is possible to obtain ten-minute tapes - five minutes each side. Record the same story on each side so that children can turn over the tape themselves. A library of 'sound' tapes could be assembled, incorporating the sound, a poem or rhyme, and a story. Parent helpers may be able to help here by recording stories, giving a variety of voices.

Aa

anorak

arrow

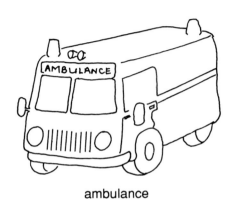

ambulance

apple

axe

a

Aa

We begin with a. Colour us.

ACTIVITIES

- Make asleep/awake pictures (see photograph).
- Print with apples. Use for borders surrounding displays.
- Make sequence patterns using apple prints of different colours.
- Cook apples in different ways - baking apples gives an excellent example of change brought about by heat.
- Look at and compare different varieties of apples.
- Collect pictures or models of animals - see how many different animals you can find.
- Examine and draw animal tracks Find an ants' nest and observe the movements of the ants.
- Addition sums - introduce the sign +, add.
- Addresses - children learn their own.
- Act as astronauts. Find suitable music, and experiment with different actions during movement lessons.
- Find paintings and pictures of acrobats.
- Talk about what ambulances do, and talk about accidents. How can we prevent these?
- Listen to part of 'Carnival of the Animals' by Saint-Saens - 'The Aquarium' would be appropriate.

● **Make aquarium pictures (see line drawing).**

Vocabulary

acrobat, accident, actor, actress, add, address, adventure, alarm (clock), alligator, alphabet, ambulance, anchor, animal, ankle, ant, apple, arrow, axe, about, above, across, asleep, awake, away.

Bb

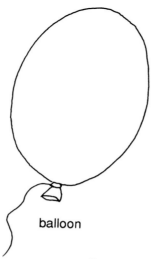

balloon

boat

bed

bell

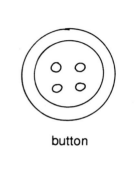

button

b

B b

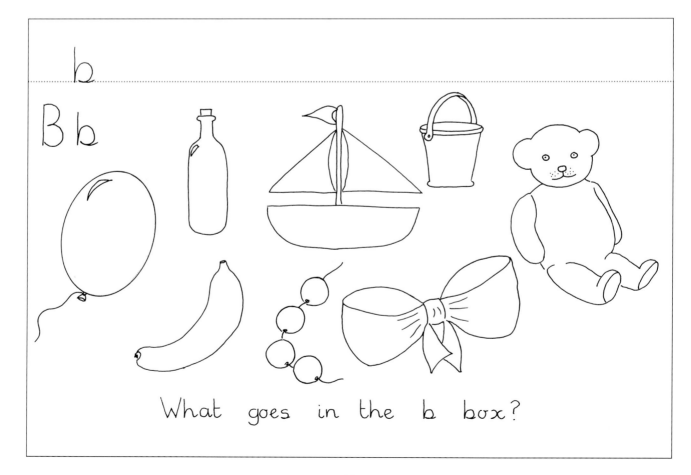

What goes in the b box?

ACTIVITIES

- Make a 'b' box - cover a cardboard box with blue paper, decorate with blue bubble prints. Fill with objects beginning with 'b' (see photograph).
- Blow bubbles.
- Make bubble prints.
- Blow up balloons - what happens when you let go of an untied balloon?
- Make butterfly prints and blot patterns.
- Sail boats on bubbly blue water in the water trolley.
- Cook biscuits and buns.
- Use buttons in number activities - such as finding how many cover a surface.
- Listen to 'Flight of the Bumblebee' by Rimsky-Korsakov.
- Make bees from cardboard cylinders.
- Birthday celebrations
- Talk about babies. If possible, ask a parent to bring in a baby to the classroom. Talk about the baby.
- Baby pictures. Children could paint pictures of babies.
- Children could bring in photographs and have a display of baby pictures. Ask other members of staff to bring in photographs of themselves as babies. Can the children match the baby with the adult?
- Play ball games: bouncing ball; ball-in-a-bucket race.
- Play bean-bag games.

- **Beetle game**

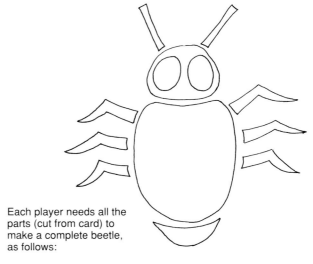

Each player needs all the parts (cut from card) to make a complete beetle, as follows:

a body - 1
a head - 2
two eyes - 3
two antennae - 4
six legs - 5
a tail - 6
Each part has a value.
Each player rolls the dice in turn - must get a body (No. l) to start, then builds up the beetle.

Vocabulary

baby, bacon, bag, baker, ball, balloon, basket, bat, bead, bean, beanbag, baked beans, bear, bed, bee, beetle, bell, berry, bicycle, bird, biscuit, boat, bone, bonnet, book, bottle, box, bubble, bucket, bus.

Cc

candle

cake

cat

castle

car

C

C c

Join the c pictures.

ACTIVITIES

- Make a picture of Clever Clown, who catches things beginning with 'c' (see photograph).
- Make coconut cakes.
- Grow carrot tops. Print with carrots.
- Make a castle - use square or oblong sponges to print the bricks.
- Make patterns with combs in very thick paint.
- Make candles from cardboard cylinders (see photograph).
- Cook cauliflower, cabbage, carrots and courgettes.
- Use conkers in mathematical activities.
- Make cards and calendars (individual, or class calendar).
- Talk about cubes and cuboids.
- Play counting games.
- **Use cake and candle shapes to make a number line** (see line drawing).

- **Collection games** - children have a basket in which they put items collected (see line drawing).

Vocabulary

cabbage, cactus, cage, cake, calendar, camel, camera, candle, cap, car, caravan, card, cardigan, carrot, castanets, castle, cat, coat, coin, cone, conker, cook, coat, cow, cowboy, cucumber, cuckoo, cupboard, curtain, call, can/cannot, catch, came, come.

one candle on the cake

two candles on the cake

three candles on the cake

four candles on the cake

Dd

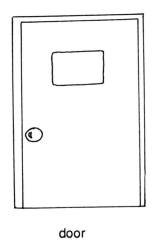

door

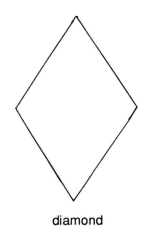

diamond

doll

dog

duck

d

Dd

Look what we found in the dustbin.

Take care ~ our dinosaurs are dangerous.

ACTIVITIES

- Make a dinosaur island (see photograph). Build up base with boxes, cover with papier mâché and finish with tissue paper.
- Make a collection of dinosaur posters and books. Make a collection of dolls, to order, compare, measure etc. Give each a label which shows its owner's name - This is Jodie's doll; Emily's doll has black hair, and so on.
- Use egg boxes to make daffodils - cut up, paint yellow and stick on to background, with yellow cut paper petals.
- Tessellate diamond shapes.
- Draw pictures of Daddy - make a class book of daddy portraits.
- Talk about doctors and dentists and what they do.
- Make dot-to-dot pictures.
- **Make door books**
(see line drawing).

- **Print with finger tips to make daisies,** using white paint for petals and yellow paint for the centre (see line drawing).

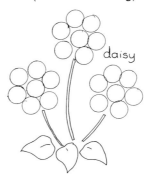

- What's in the dustbin? Collect items to put in the dustbin - either beginning with 'd' (doll, duck, dog, dinosaur, diamond) or having a common property (e.g. all red). This activity could be related to science, and discussion about waste.

Vocabulary

daddy, daffodil, daisy, desk, diamond, diary, dinosaur, dish, diver, doctor, dog, doll, donkey, door, duck, dance, dig, do.

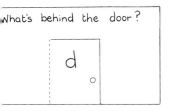

Ee

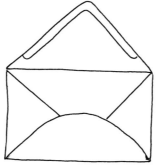

envelope

elephant

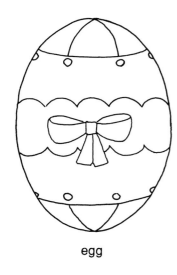

egg

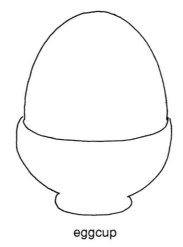

eggcup

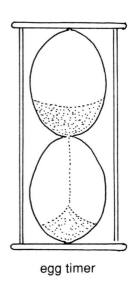

egg timer

e

E e

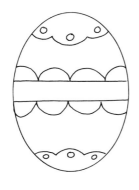

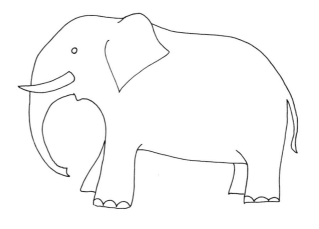

Egg and elephant begin with e.

Elmer lives in the jungle where it is hot.

Elmer is an elephant.

ACTIVITIES

- Read the story of Elmer the Elephant, and make a class picture about him. Tessellate tissue paper squares to make Elmer's patch-work skin (see photograph).
- Cook eggs in different ways.
- Hard boil eggs in water containing either edible food colouring or natural dyes: outer skin of onions - brown; raw beetroot - red/pink. Masking tape can be applied before dyeing to give a striped effect, or try winding dental floss round the eggs.
- Make egg shell pictures.
- Make a collection of pictures of things which work by electricity. Discuss uses and dangers.
- Find exit and entrance signs around the school.
- Talk about exciting things. What do the children find exciting?
- Collect envelopes - large, small, coloured - make a collage.
- Use an egg-timer to time activities.
- Talk about exercise - how we all need it to keep fit and healthy.
- Look at models and pictures of engines.

- **Make an eggosaurus** - an imaginary dinosaur made from an egg box (see line drawing).

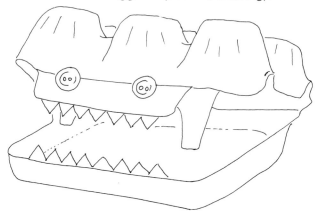

- Play the echo game using percussion instruments - teacher or child plays short rhythm sequence, which is then copied, or 'echoed'.

Vocabulary

egg, elephant, eleven, elf, empty, end, engine, entrance, exit, envelope, escape, Eskimo, everybody, everyone, every, exercise.

Ff

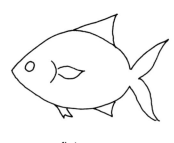

fish

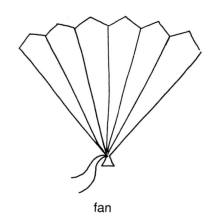

fan

feather

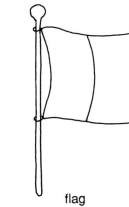

flag

flower

f

F f

fish

flag

flower

feather

4 four

fan

ACTIVITIES

- Make funny faces (see photograph).
- Paint with feathers.
- Make paper fans.
- Footprints - compare the size of children's feet, and make footprint picture on a large piece of paper spread on the floor.
- Talk about fire fighters. If possible, look at a fire engine.
- Finger paint.
  Use different techniques, for example printing directly on paper, or taking a print from a pattern on a work surface.
- Make foil fish - display as mobiles.
- Make flags.
- Cook fairy cakes.
- Paint fire pictures - black background with red/orange/yellow tissue, foil and crêpe paper.
- Make books about families. Bring in photographs of children's families. (These could be photocopied for use in children's own books.)
- Play 'happy family' card games.
- Play with toy farm and farm animals. Talk about the work of a farmer.
- Play follow-my-leader.
- **Play a 'fishing' game,** using 'f' words (see line drawing).

Vocabulary

face, fairy, family, fan, farm, farmer, father, feather, fence, field, finger, fire, fish, five, fog, foot, football, forest, fork, four, fox.

Gg

gate

glove

garage

guitar

girl

g

Gg

glove

guitar

goose

girl

garage

gate

We all begin with g. Colour us.

ACTIVITIES

- **Make 'Go through the garden gate' pictures**
  (see photograph).

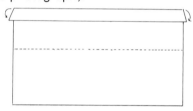

I. Fold paper in half and open out. Fold back one end to form hedge and gate.

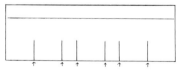

2. Refold paper. Cut into folded edge - do not remove any paper.

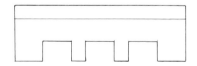

3. Open and fold each 'box' on itself, then refold the whole card.

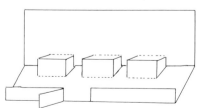

4. Stand open. Cut out gate in hedge. Glue house and flowers to leading face of cut-outs. Draw trees on background and hedge or fence on front flap.

- Look at gardens in your own area, or go to a public park.
- Make an indoor garden on a tray
- Listen to guitar music.
- Borrow a guitar - look at its shape, talk about how it is played etc. Make observational drawings of a guitar.
- Make 'goldfish in the bowl' pictures.
- Make glove puppets - old socks make an excellent base for these.
- Match a glove to its pair.
- Talk about different sorts of gloves - make a collection (boxing gloves, gardening gloves, oven gloves etc).
- Design a pair of gloves. Draw around hands and draw or paint your designs on the shapes.
- Guessing games, e.g. teacher gives clues such as 'it has five fingers', 'it keeps my hands warm', 'it can be made of wool', etc.
- Make a garage from found materials for a set of tiny cars.
- Make a bridge to carry the Billy Goats Gruff across the river to the green grass.

Vocabulary

game, garage, garden, gate, ghost, gift, girl, goat, goblin, gold, goldfish, gorilla, guinea pig, guitar, gull, giggle, go.

Hh

heart

hat

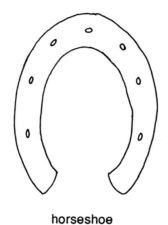

house

horseshoe

holly

h

Hh

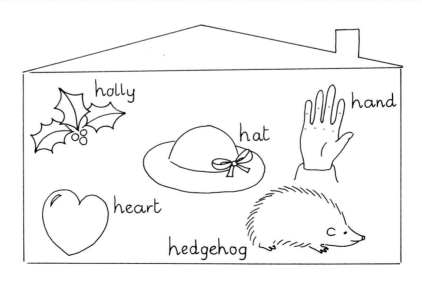

What is in the h house?

28

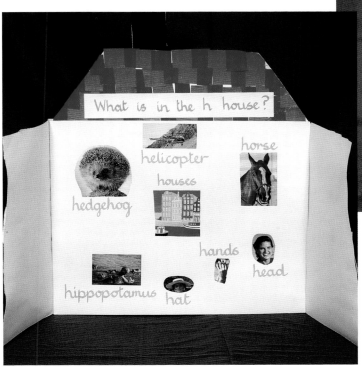

ACTIVITIES

- Make a 'h' house (see photograph). Pictures could be drawn by children, or cut from magazines.
- Holidays. Where would you like to go on holiday?
- Collect different sorts of hats for a display (sun hat, rain hat, trilby etc).
- Make hats from found materials.
- Make happy faces - can be made quickly using paper plates. Use as puppets, masks or mobiles.
- Make hedgehogs from Plasticine, play dough, or bread dough with almond 'spines'. (These can be baked to make hedgehog rolls to be eaten with honey.)
- Turn the play area into a hospital.
- Look at children's hair colour - make a graph to show differences.
- Why do people wear helmets? Make a collection, either real, or photographs.
- Talk about different kinds of houses and homes. Match animals to their homes.
- Look at pictures of horses - talk about hooves and horseshoes.
- Play hopscotch.
- Play hopping games.

- **Make handprints.** Use these for borders, giving an opportunity for sequencing; or cut out and make into pictures: green for a tree, brown/yellow for a lion's mane, white for a swan, etc. - see line drawing).

Vocabulary

hair, half, ham, hammer, hamster, hand, hat, head, heart, hedge, hedgehog, helmet, hen, hill, hippopotamus, holiday, holly, home, honey, hop, horse, hot, house, here, help.

29

ill

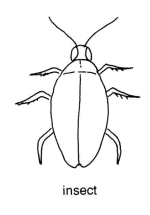

insect

igloo

ink

in

i

I i

Where is it? Look for the insect 🐝

 is it in here?

 is it in here?

 is it in here?

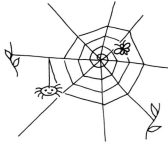 is it in here?

30

My ink-blot looked like a pond.

My ink-blot looked like under the sea.

My ink-blot looked like the sea.

We blew at ink through a straw.

My ink-blot looked like a birthday cake.

My ink-blot looked like a spider.

My ink-blot looked like a bush.

ACTIVITIES

- Make ink pictures - by blowing ink into shapes (see photograph).
- Look at and taste Indian breads. Other kinds of Indian food could be cooked (e.g dahl).
- Observe insects. Go for a walk around the school grounds to look for insects.
- Make a group picture about Incy Wincy Spider.
- Talk about invitations - make a collection of different kinds - wedding, party, etc.
- Look at musical instruments - listen to the sounds they make.
- Just imagine - explain the meaning of the word 'imagine'. Make a class book of imaginary situations, animals etc.
- What do children find interesting?
- What's inside? Make rattles from tins or plastic containers with different materials inside - rice/sand/pebbles. Play guessing games, or games matching pairs of rattles.

- **Look at little words which begin with 'i'** - if, in, is, it - see if you can find them in big words - sister, little, into, lift (see line drawing).

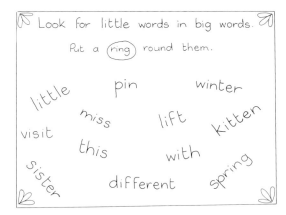

Look for little words in big words.

Put a (ring) round them.

little   pin   winter

    miss   lift   kitten

visit

    this   with   spring

sister   different

Vocabulary

ill, igloo, Indian, indoors, infant, ink, insect, inside, invitation, itch, is, it, in, if, into, imagine.

J j

jam

jumper

jelly

Jack-in-the-box

jug

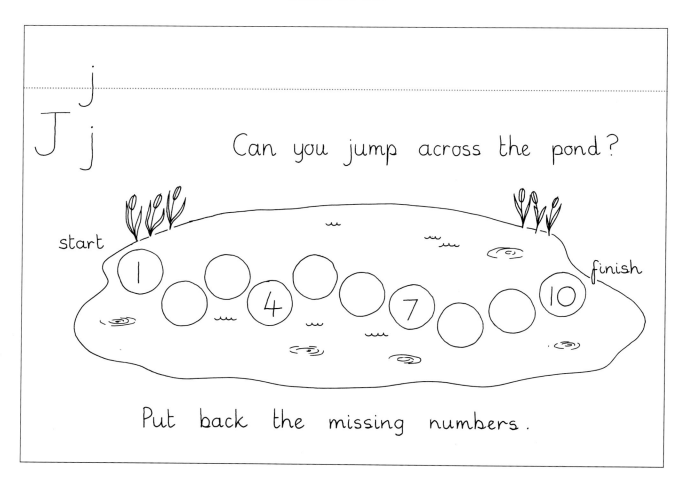

J j
J j

Can you jump across the pond?

start

finish

Put back the missing numbers.

Come to our jammy jelly party!

When we mixed red jelly and yellow jelly we made orange jelly. ⬤ and ⬤ made

ACTIVITIES

● Make jelly and Jammy Circles (see recipe on page 70) or jam tarts. Have a Jammy Jelly party (see photograph).

● What happens when we mix different coloured jellies? Use different shaped containers. Why do we put jelly in a fridge?

● Play with jigsaws - try making jigsaws.

● Make a collection of jugs - look at different shapes, colours, sizes and materials. Make observational drawings of jugs.

● Find pictures of jelly fish.

● **Make 'jelly fish' from lidded plastic pots** turned upside down, or polystyrene trays. Experiment with different packaging items to see which float well. Add string 'tentacles' (see line drawing).

● Listen to some jazz music.

● What do we mean by a joke? Can you think of a good joke to tell your friends? Make a collection of favourite jokes.

● Talk about jungles - which animals might you find there? What is a jungle like? Make a jungle picture or use crêpe and tissue paper mobiles to transform the classroom into a jungle.

● Make Jack-in-the-boxes from found materials.

● Play jumping games

● How many jelly beans are there? **Play a game of estimation.**

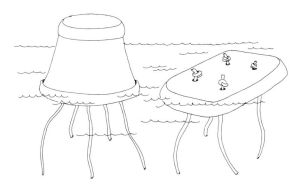

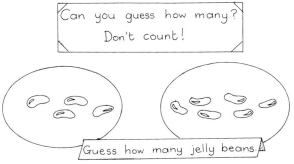

Can you guess how many? Don't count!

Guess how many jelly beans.

Vocabulary

Jack-in-the-box, jacket, jam, January, jar, jelly, jeans, jersey, jet, jewel, jigsaw, jug, juice, jump, jumper, June, July.

Kk

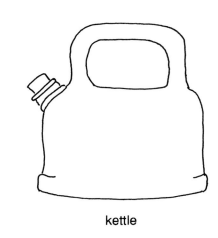

kangaroo

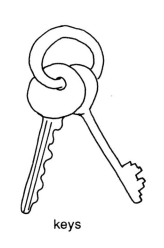

kettle

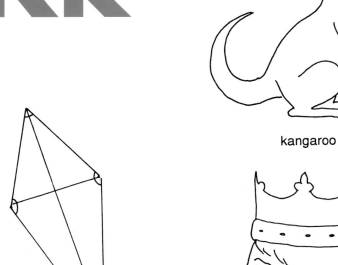

kite

king

keys

k

Kk

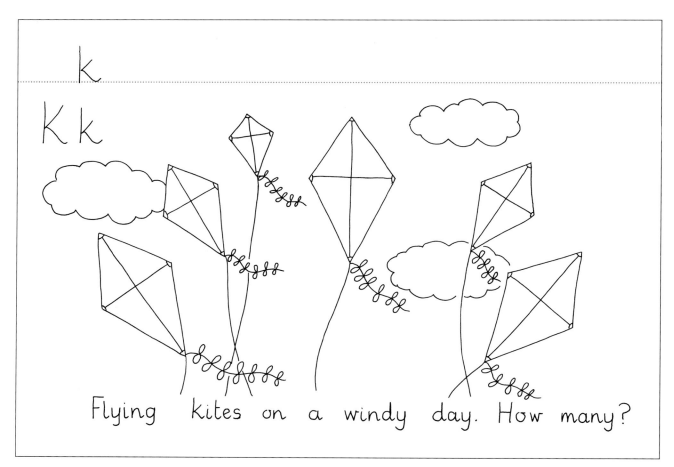

Flying kites on a windy day. How many?

ACTIVITIES
● Make kites to fly on a windy day (see photograph).

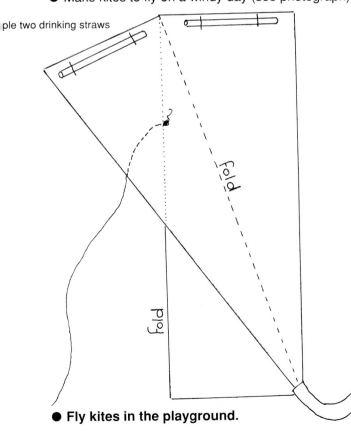

ple two drinking straws

fold

fold

● **Fly kites in the playground.**

Add a ribbon tail and string.

● Look at kaleidoscopes.
● Make a collection of keys - try to find different sorts, old and new, large and small.
● Make key rubbings.
● Find pictures or photographs of animals and birds whose names begin with 'k' - kangaroo, koala bear, kitten, kid, kingfisher, kookaburra, kiwi.
● Turn the play area into a kitchen. Provide appropriate equipment. Talk about hygiene in the kitchen.
● Look at different kinds of kettles - old and new.
● Make crowns and act as kings.
● Talk about kindness - ask the children for ideas on how they can be kind to others. Make a class book.
● Listen to 'The Karelia Suite' by Sibelius.
● Kick footballs.

Vocabulary
kangaroo, kennel, ketchup, kettle, key, kick, kid, king, kitchen, kite, kitten, koala bear, kiwi, kookaburra.

Ll

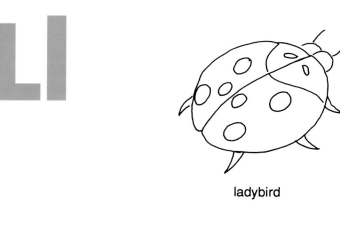

ladybird

lollipop

ladder

leaf

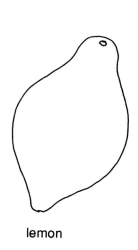

lemon

l

L l

All our names begin with L. Colour us.

Ladybird, Ladybird,
fly away home.

ACTIVITIES

- Make a ladybird picture (see photograph).
- See how many different kinds of leaves you can find - sort and compare them; make leaf prints; press leaves; make a collage combining pressed and printed leaves.
- Use orange, brown and yellow handprints to make the mane of a lion.
- Look at lemons - smell and taste, then use to make lemon flavoured biscuits and cakes.
- Discuss length: long, longer, longest. Compare lengths.
- **Make lanterns.**
- Make a graph of favourite lollipop flavours.
- Write letters - provide envelopes for children's letters.
- Put up a washing line in the play area - use for sequencing activities.
- Make lists of things that children like (about themselves, school, the playground).
- Play the game 'I sent a letter to my love....'

Vocabulary

label, ladder, lady, lake, lamb, lamp, lantern, land, leaf, leather, leg, lemon, lemonade, letter, lettuce, lid, light, line, lion, lip, lobster, lollipop, laugh.

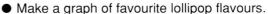

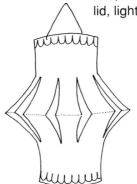

Mm

mittens

marble

mouse

mushroom

monkey

m

M m   Draw mummy in your home.

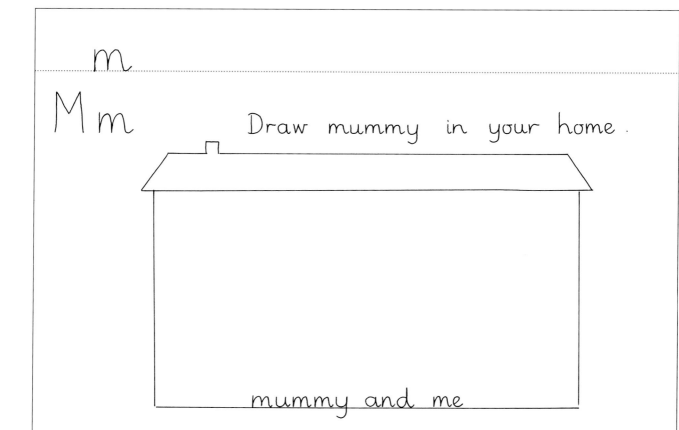

mummy and me

We made mouse masks.

ACTIVITIES

- Make mouse masks (see photograph). Encourage the children to use them in impromptu play situations.
- Make moon mobiles - moon shapes in the different phases would add interest.
- Listen to 'The Moonlight Sonata' by Beethoven.
- Introduce activities using magnets and magnifying glasses.
- Talk about markets - visit one if possible and turn the play area into a market stall. Use this as a starting point for money activities.
- **Match mittens.**

- Make marbling patterns, either by taking prints from oil paint floating on water, or by rolling marbles across paint-spattererd paper.

- Look at milk. Talk about where it comes from, what we use it for, its value in a balanced diet.
- Taste marmalade - try several different kinds.
- Draw pictures of Mummy - make a class book of mummy portraits.
- **Make maraccas,** using squeezy bottles or tins. Use them to accompany singing or poems.

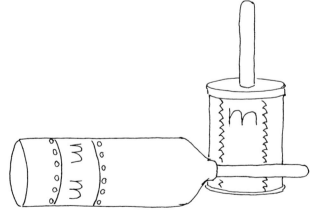

- Play marble games.

Vocabulary

machine, magic, man, map, marble, March, May, market, mat, meadow, melon, mermaid, milk, mirror, mitten, money, moon, morning, moth, mother, mountain, mouth, mud, mug, mummy.

Nn

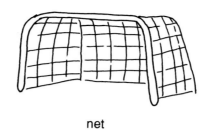
net

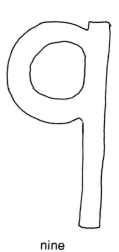
nine

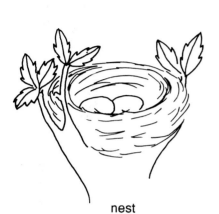
nest

night

necklace

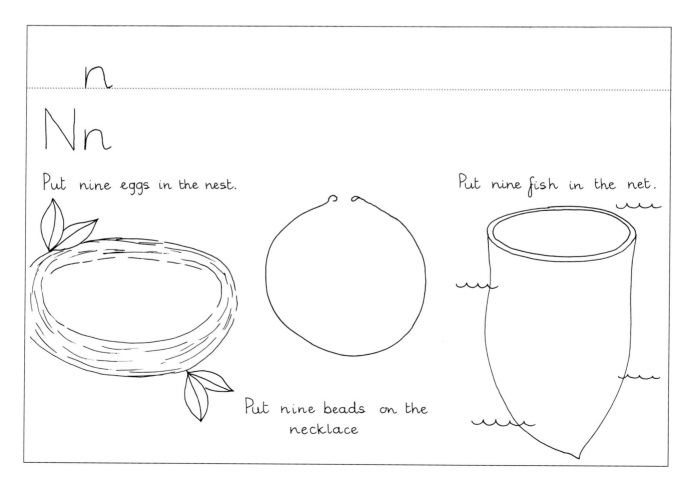

n

Nn

Put nine eggs in the nest.

Put nine fish in the net.

Put nine beads on the necklace

40

ACTIVITIES

- Make a night-time picture (see photograph). Discuss what night is like. Draw a scene with wax crayons and give it a dark blue wash.
- Talk about nocturnal animals. Why do they come out at night?
- Talk about names - how many names has each child? Explain terms 'surname' and 'forename'. Clap the rhythm of each child's name.
- Make nurses' hats and use them in dramatic play.
- How many kinds of nets can you think of (fishing, hair, vegetable, tennis etc)?
- Listen to 'The Nutcracker Suite', Tchaikovsky.
- Look at a bird's nest (abandoned). See how it is constructed. Make observational drawings.
- **Make necklaces** - use beads or drinking straws cut into short lengths. Encourage sequence patterns.

- Look for numbers on houses, road signs, buses etc.
- **Make number mobiles** - children decorate numbers 1-10. This can then be used as a number line.

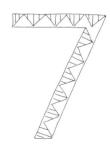

- Play ninepins.
- Play noughts and crosses.

Vocabulary

nail, neck, necklace, needle, net, nest, newspaper, niece, night, nine, nose, number, nurse, nut, not, no, nip.

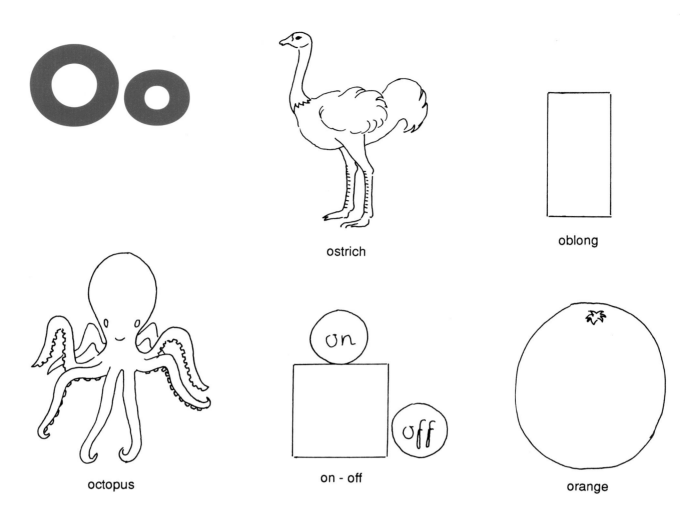

ostrich

oblong

octopus

on - off

orange

octopus

oblong

ostrich

orange

We begin with o. Colour us.

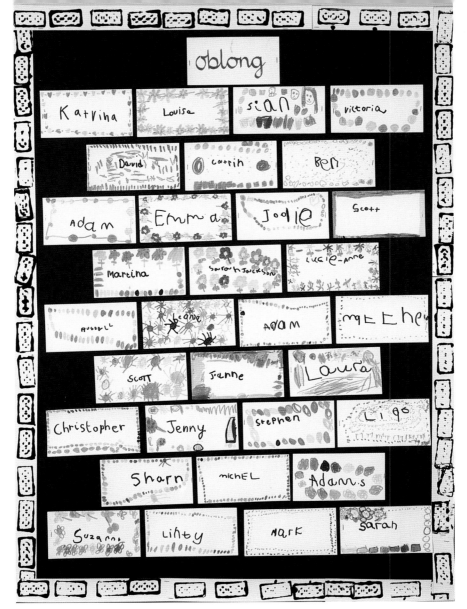

ACTIVITIES

- Make an oblong name wall - children write name on an oblong, and decorate (see photograph).
- Visit the school office - talk to the secretary about office work, then turn the play area into an office.
- Make orange jelly and orange biscuits.
- Talk about 'on' and 'off'.
- Use shades and tints of orange to make pictures - add tissue, crêpe and Cellophane to give texture.
- Look at pictures or photographs of ostriches and otters.
- Think of as many opposites as possible.
- Listen to 'The Love of Three Oranges' by Prokofiev.
- **Tessellate oblongs.**

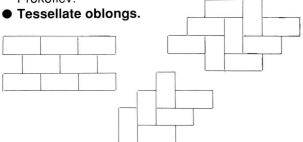

- **Make an underwater scene** with an octopus among the sea creatures.

- Play Odd Man Out. This game can take different forms - from simple, e.g. a blue object amongst all red objects; to more complicated, e.g. four animal pictures - cow, pig, lion, horse; OR, play Rhyming Odd Man Out, e.g. pen, men, met, den; OR Alliterative Odd Man Out, e.g. bat, bun, pet, ball.

Vocabulary

oblong, octopus, October, off, on, office, orange, ostrich, otter.

Pp

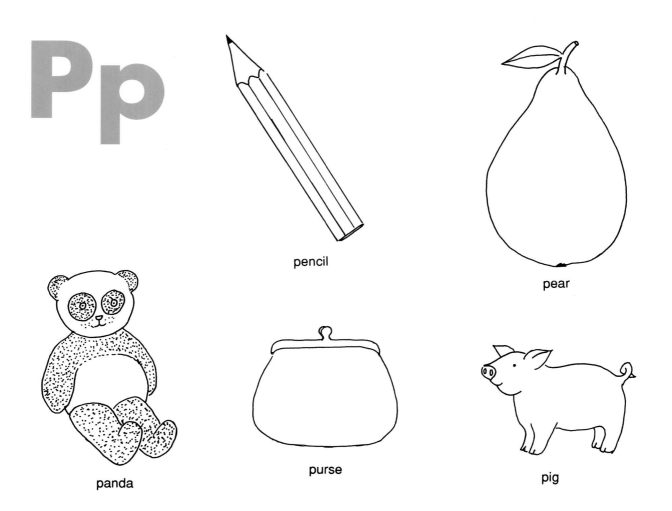

pencil

pear

panda

purse

pig

p

P p

Colour the pigs pink and purple.

Our puppets' names begin with p.

Peter · Penny · Polly · Pat

ACTIVITIES

- Make puppet people (see photograph). Give each puppet a name beginning with 'p'.
- Paint pink and purple pictures.
- Print with potatoes.
- Make pipe cleaner people and peg dolls.
- Talk about the pets that children may have at home. Do a class survey and display as a graph of some kind.
- Pop popcorn and make pancakes, pastry people and porridge.
- Use torn paper to make pictures.
- Collect postcards. Make a display of holiday postcards.
- Make tissue paper poppies.
- Look at photographs and pictures of parrots. Perhaps you could make a colourful mobile display of different parrots.
- Put all equipment necessary for a picnic in the play area - a real picnic in the school grounds would be fun.
- Make the play area into a post office with posters, postcards, stamps, parcels, packages, and so on.
- Collect pebbles - see how many colours and sizes you can find.
- Talk about police. Invite a policeman to talk to the children.
- Listen to 'The Pizzicato Polka' by Delibes and 'Playful Pizzicato' by Benjamin Britten.
- **Make penguins** from found materials.

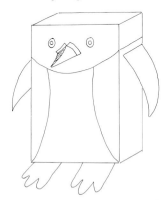

- Play 'pass the parcel'.

Vocabulary

packet, paddle, page, paint, palace, pan, pancake, panda, pantomime, paper, parachute, parcel, parrot, party, passenger, patch, path, pattern, pavement, pea, peach, peacock, peanut, pear, pebble, pedal, peel, peg, pelican, pen, pencil, pet, pig, pin, pink.

Qq

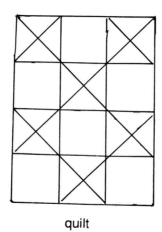

quilt

queen

question mark

quack

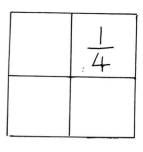

quarter

qu

Qu qu

Five little ducks went out to play.

Pussy-cat, pussy-cat
Where have you been?
I've been up to London
To visit the Queen.
Pussy-cat, pussy-cat
What did you there?
I frightened a
little mouse
Under her chair.

queen

ACTIVITIES

- Paint pictures of queens and make a picture of Pussycat, Pussycat (see photograph).
- Listen to 'The Arrival of the Queen of Sheba' by Handel.
- Make crowns and act as queens.
- Talk about occasions when we need to be quiet - children draw or paint pictures to make wall display.
- Make a quilt of coloured paper or material shapes. Tessellate the different shapes (see photograph on page 5 for 'a').
- Talk about questions and question marks.
- What happens during an earthquake? Find photographs and pictures to show what an earthquake can do.
- What sound does a duck make? Pretend to be ducks in movement lessons.
- Compare quick/slow movements.
- Talk about quarrels. What happens to start a quarrel? How should we behave to stop quarrels from happening?

- **Fold a piece of paper into four to make quarters** - practise writing 'qu' in each quarter and then decorate.

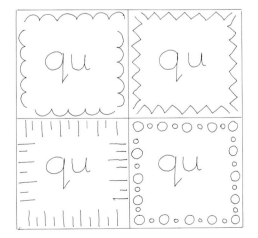

Vocabulary

quack, quarter, quarrel, queen, question, quiver, quiet, quilt, quick, queue.

Rr

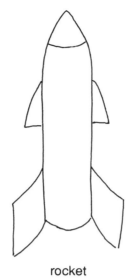

rocket

roof

rabbit

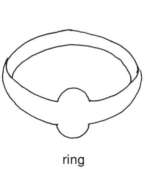

ring

rocking horse

r

R r

Finish the robot.

ACTIVITIES

- Make robots from found materials. Display on a red background (see photograph).
- Make rattles from tins/yoghurt pots - use to accompany songs.
- Make rockets from cardboard cylinders.
- Make cakes from a rice-based cereal. Add some raisins for another 'r' word. Talk about the word 'recipe'.
- Cook rice. Look at it before and after cooking.
- Make a red display. Include pictures, using a variety of techniques.
- Make rubbings. In the playground: bricks, the playground surface, tree bark. In the classroom: coins, buttons, paper-clips.
- Make rainbow pictures. Talk about the colours in a rainbow and when we might see one.
- Use 'ragging' to make backgrounds for pictures. (Crumple a piece of fabric and dab it over a painted surface.)
- Make a fairground roundabout from found materials.
- Run races.

- **Make robins** - these look effective as mobiles.

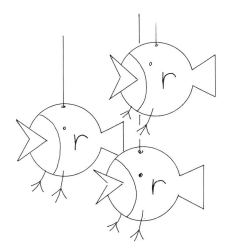

Vocabulary

rabbit, race, radio, rag, rail, rain, rainbow, raisin, rat, rattle, read, recipe, record, recorder, red, rhinoceros, ribbon, rice, ring, road, robin, rock, rocket, rocking-horse, roller skate, roof, room, rose, roundabout, run.

Ss

sausage

scissors

snowman

sun

snail

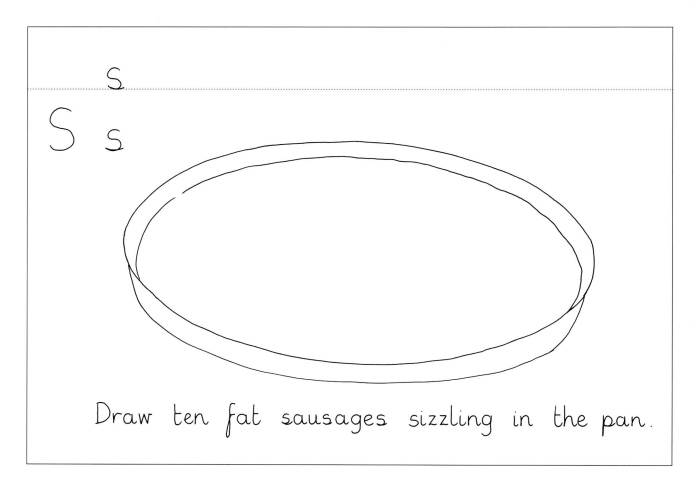

S

S s

Draw ten fat sausages sizzling in the pan.

ACTIVITIES

● Look at 'Sunflowers' by Van Gogh. Use thick paint to make own sunflower paintings. (See photograph. Recipe for paint is on page 70.)

● Examine sunflowers. Grow sunflower plants from seed.

● Talk about the sun and the seasons.

● Make smiling faces - display as mobiles.

● Use silver foil to make rubbings - place foil over the object and rub gently with finger tips. Make silver collage pictures with the rubbings.

● Collect pictures of things beginning with 's' and make an 's' scrapbook.

● Sand play.

● Add salt to paint to give it a granular texture (see cover artwork).

● Make a seaside picture - see how many 's' words you can include - sky, sun, seaweed, sandcastle, seagull etc.

● **Make Slippery Sam puppets** from an old sock.

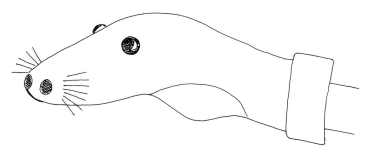

● What is special about Saturday and Sunday?

● **Make a 'snake box'** - upturned shoe box with snakes, some long, some short, slotted through the base. A long snake, when pulled out, makes a long 'sssss...'; a short snake, a short 'sss..'

● Play skipping games.
● Play Snap card games.

Vocabulary

sack, sad, sail, sand, sausage, school, sea, see, seed, seven, silver, sister, sit, six, small, snake, snow, snowman, soap, spider, star, stick, stop, sun, summer, spring, swim.

T t

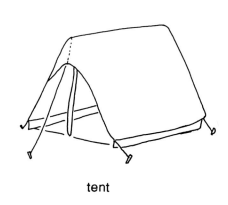

television

tent

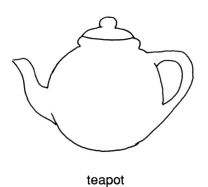

teapot

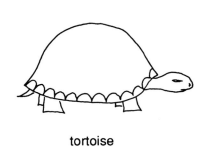

tortoise

table

t

T t

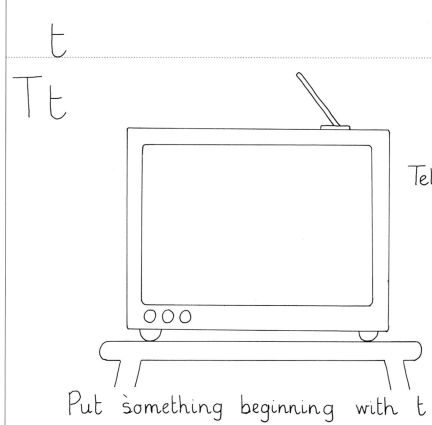

Television on the table.

Put something beginning with t on television.

ACTIVITIES

- What's on the 't' television? (See photograph.)
- Make tea and toast.
- Talk on toy telephones.
- Make a collection of children's favourite toys. With teacher as scribe, write about why they chose their toy.
- Play tambourines and tambors.
- Look at pictures and photographs of tigers.
- Make a tent in your play area. Use a big sheet supported in some way. (The sheet could be decorated by printing, perhaps with the letter shape 't'.)
- Talk about teeth and toothbrushes. Explain the importance of oral hygiene - make a display of dental cleaning equipment.
- Talk about tadpoles.
- **Make individual pull-through televisions.**

- Listen to 'Toccata and Fugue in D Minor' by Bach.
- When do we have to buy tickets? Make a collection, and put these in a book (perhaps with an explanation about each event).
- **Make a teddy who only eats things which begin with 't'.**

Vocabulary

table, tadpole, tail, tambourine, tap, tape, tart, tassel, taxi, tea, teacher, teddy bear, tooth, telephone, telescope, television, two, ten, tent, ticket, tiger, toast, toffee, town.

Uu

umbrella - up

umbrella - down

sun umbrella

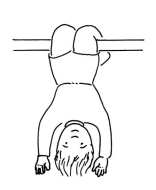

upside-down

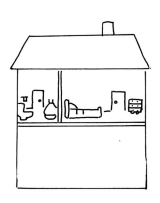

upstairs

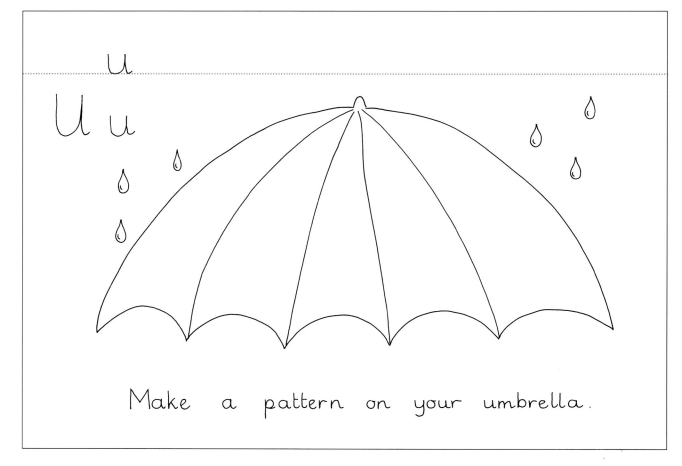

u

U u

Make a pattern on your umbrella.

ACTIVITIES

● Make 'under my umbrella' pictures (see photograph).

> Up goes my umbrella as down comes the rain.
> I am keeping dry 'til the sun comes out again.
> Under my umbrella on a wet and windy day,
> I am keeping dry 'til the rainclouds roll away.

● Talk about uncles - how many uncles does each child have? Make a class survey.
● Make a collection of umbrellas - large/small, beach, golf, different colours etc.
● Look at 'Les Parapluis' by Renoir.
● In movement, explore under/over, and up/down.
● What happens underground? Talk about animals who live underground, and about underground tunnels, pipes, mines, etc.
● Look up in the sky - what might we see there (clouds, sun, moon, aeroplane, hot air balloons, birds, etc.)?
● Talk about underclothes. Why do we call them underclothes? Collect and make a display of different sorts.
● Play under and over - obstacle race.
● Unwrap each layer in 'pass the parcel'.
● Umbrella game - open an umbrella, balance it upside down and try throwing balls into it.

● **Make a dolls' house with an upstairs.** What is upstairs in a house? Use dolls' house furniture to illustrate.

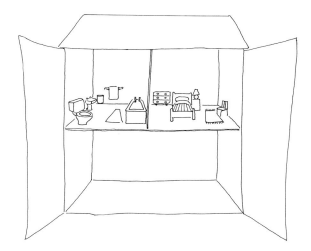

Vocabulary

ugly, umbrella, under, uncle, underwater, underground, unwrap, up, upstairs, upon, upset, undo, understand, unlucky, untidy, unusual, upside-down.

V v

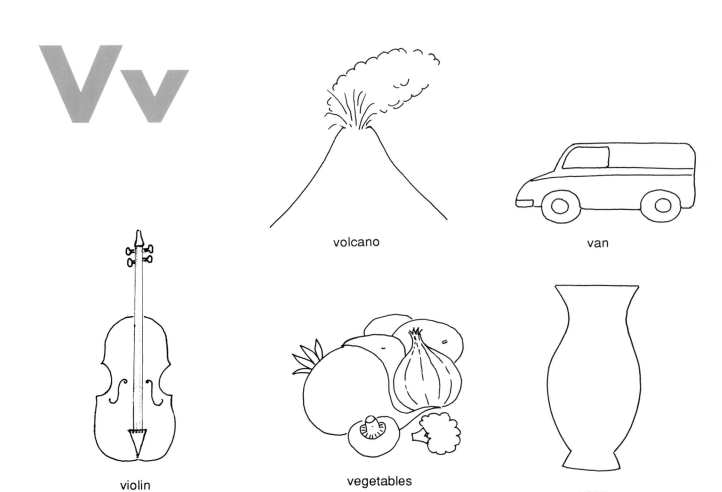

volcano

van

violin

vegetables

vase

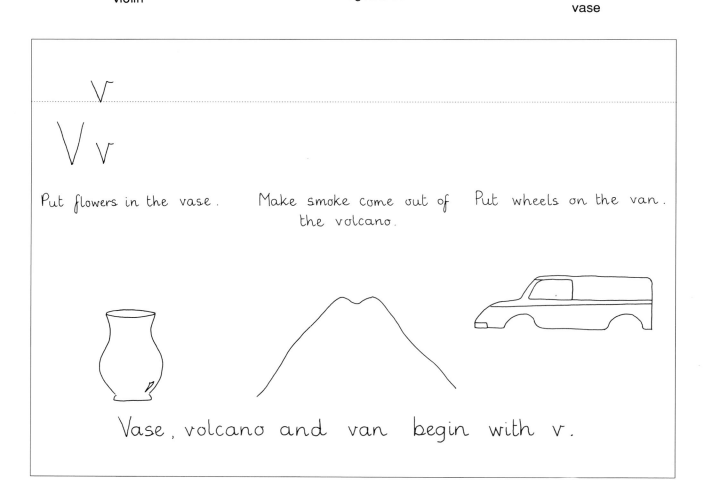

V

V v

Put flowers in the vase.   Make smoke come out of the volcano.   Put wheels on the van.

Vase, volcano and van begin with v.

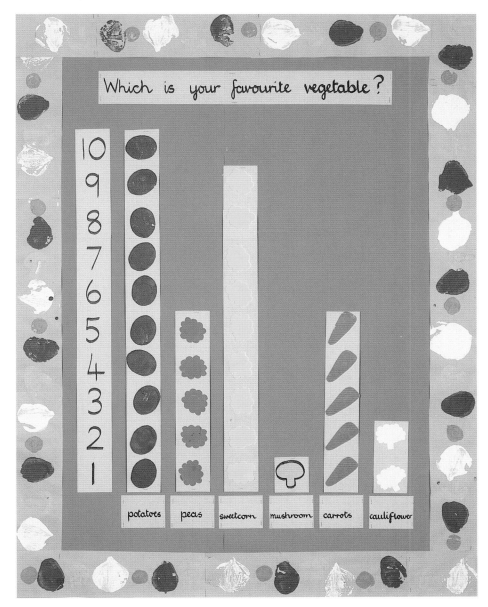

Which is your favourite vegetable?

potatoes	peas	sweetcorn	mushroom	carrots	cauliflower

ACTIVITIES

- Talk about vegetables - make a block graph of children's favourite vegetables (see photograph).
- Make a collection of vegetables. Where do they grow? Which part do we eat? etc.
- Use vegetables in cookery - vegetable soup requires group work, cutting up carrots, onions, etc.
- Print with vegetables (see display border above). Onions cut vertically and horizontally give interesting patterns.
- What is a volcano? What happens when a volcano erupts? Interpreting a volcanic eruption in music and movement is a stimulating activity. ('Mars' from the Planet Suite is suitable music to use.)
- Borrow a violin - examine it carefully. Try drawing it, and listen to the sounds it makes.
- Talk about Valentine's Day - make cards.
- Smell vinegar and vanilla - what do the smells make you think of?

- **Make a vase**. Use a washing-up liquid bottle (with neck cut off) as a base. Cover with torn newspaper soaked in cold water paste until there is a thick layer. Cover with white paper and, when dry, decorate. Add buttons or sequins. Varnish with diluted PVA glue. The bottle can be left in, making it possible to use the vase for real flowers.

Vocabulary

vacuum, valley, van, Valentine, vanilla, vase, vegetable, velvet, vest, village, violin, violet, volcano, vulture.

watch

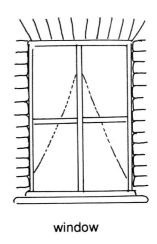

window

windmill

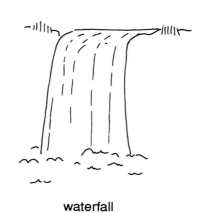

waterfall

wall

W

W w

Put some flowers in the window boxes.

What can you see through my window?

ACTIVITIES
- Make 'through my window' pictures (see photograph).
- Make weather observations - especially wet and windy weather.
- Water play - experiment with floating, sinking, capacity, displacement, etc.
- Make a collection of things with wheels. What happens when you push and pull them? Are some surfaces better than others for this?
- Make a wall for Humpty Dumpty to sit on.
- Design and make wallpaper.
- Wet paintings - brush water on to paper, then paint a picture.
- Use wool (preferably thick) to make collage pictures.
- Plant window boxes.
- Weddings - make a collection of photographs. Some children may have been bridesmaids or pageboys.
- Listen to 'The Water Music' by Handel.
- Make a friendship or name wall (see photograph on page 43).
- **Make windmills** to spin on a windy day.

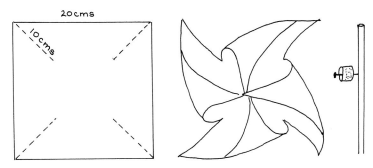

- Play What's the time, Mr. Wolf?

Vocabulary
wagon, walk, wall, wallpaper, washing, water, wave, wax, weather, web, wedding, week, well, wigwam, wind, windmill, wing, winter, witch, wolf, word, wool, worm, went, want.

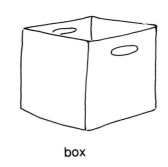
box

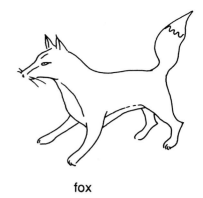
fox

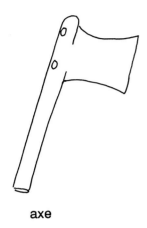
axe

box

six

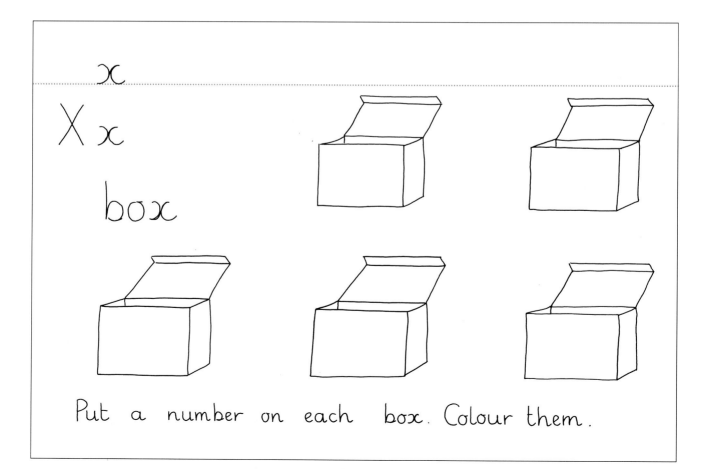

x

X x

box

Put a number on each box. Colour them.

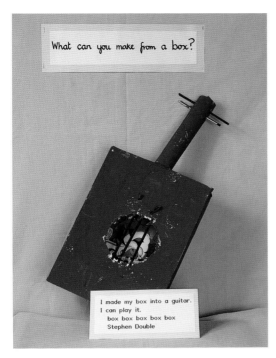

What can you make from a box?

I made my box into a guitar.
I can play it.
box box box box box
Stephen Double

I made my box into a
carry-cot.
A doll can sleep in it.
box box box box box
Sarah Jackson

I made my box into a car.
A little red teddy is riding in it.
box box box box box
Victoria Myhill

I made my box into a boat.
It will sail on the sea.
box box box box box
Louise Maxwell

ACTIVITIES

- What can you make with a box (house, carry-cot for a doll, car, robot. etc)? (See photographs.)
- Collect boxes of different shapes and sizes - investigate the net of a box by undoing and flattening it.
- Decorate boxes and make a box display, building it into an abstract 3D picture.
- Add to six.
- Make wax resist paintings.
- Make a collection of wax candles.
- Mixing - set up an activity so that children can mix paints and investigate colours. Try mixing other materials - playdough for example. Cookery involves mixing - talk about mixing as children stir ingredients.
- Look at pictures and photographs of foxes.
- What comes next? Play a memory game. Arrange objects in a line: look, cover and uncover one by one. Who can remember what comes next?

- **Make a 'six' display.**

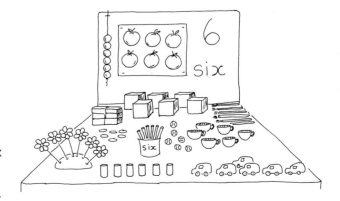

Vocabulary

axe, box, fix, fox, mix, six, wax, exit, next, taxi, sixty, excite, expect, oxygen, explain, explode, explore, express, sixteen.

Yy

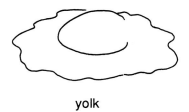

yoghurt

yolk

yellow

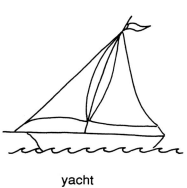

yacht

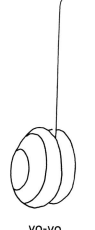

yo-yo

Y y
Y y

Can you colour the flowers yellow?

Words we know which begin with

yell Y yacht
yes year yummy
zap yes yo-yo
you yawn YELLOW
yogurt yolk yesterday

ACTIVITIES

- Make a yellow display using paints, and collage (see photograph).
- Mix tones of yellow - use yellow/white and yellow/black paint.
- Make yoghurt.
- Collect yoghurt pots - see how many different varieties you can find.
- Talk about yesterday - practise the order of days.
- When, and why, do we yawn?
- Use eggs in cookery, and examine the yellow yolk. Hardboil eggs - compare the cooked and uncooked versions. Make the boiled eggs into egg sandwiches for a picnic.
- Use yeast in breadmaking.
- Look at pictures or photographs of yaks.
- Play with yo-yos. Find out how they work.
- Play 'yes' and 'no' games.
- Play Hokey-Cokey ('You put your right arm in...').

- **Make yellow daffodils** from egg-box sections and paper.

- Talk about the year and its seasons.

Vocabulary

yawn, year, yeast, yellow, yes, yesterday, yolk, you, yoghurt, yacht, yell, yet, yo-yo, young.

Zz

zebra

zig-zag

zebra crossing

zip

buzz

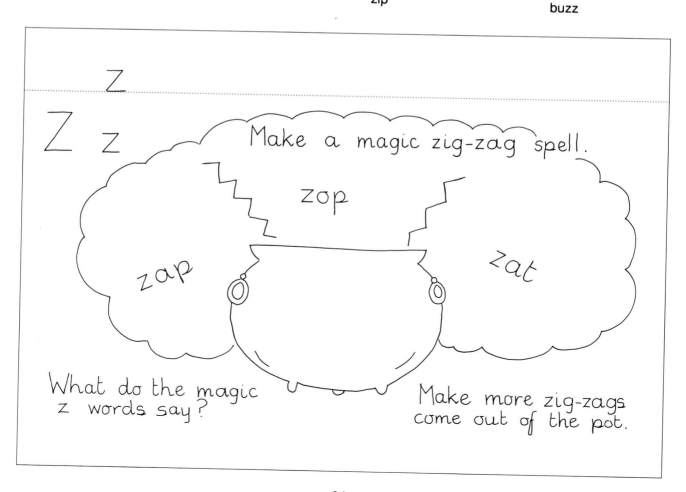

Z

Z z

Make a magic zig-zag spell.

zop

zap

zat

What do the magic z words say?

Make more zig-zags come out of the pot.

ACTIVITIES

- Make a rocket picture with count-down from ten to zero. Have zig-zag flames and smoke coming from the rocket. Explain the word 'zero'. (See photograph.)
- Look at pictures and photographs of zebras.
- Make a list of words which end in 'z' - fizz, buzz, jazz, quiz, whiz.
- Ask children to invent words beginning with 'z' - perhaps to describe a magic spell. Make a book of magic spells. The magic words must begin with 'z'.
- Make a collection of clothes which are fastened by zips. What else is fastened with zips?
- Talk about zoos - play with zoo animals. Could we plan a zoo layout which is kind to animals? Explain the important conservation work done by many zoos.
- Make zig-zag patterns with paint, crayons or felt-tip pens.
- In cookery, make pizzas. Experiment with different bases as well as different toppings.
- Make zig-zag books.

- Talk about zebra crossings and how we use them. **Make a group picture of a zebra crossing.**

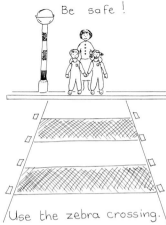

- Zooming rockets. See how far a paper rocket will fly.

Vocabulary
zebra, zero, zig-zag, zoo, zoom, zip.

65

Write the letter in the circle.

t a m s h

Which is the odd man out?

Colour the picture if its name begins with

C

Join the picture and the letter.

Join the two which begin with the same sound.

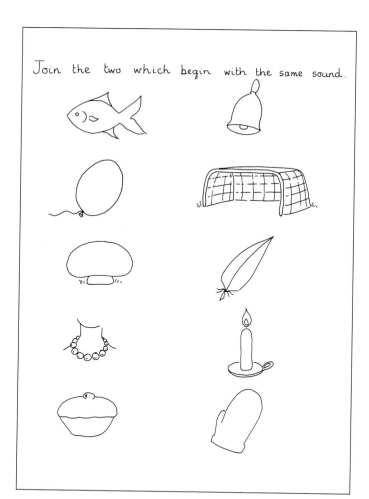

Put a (ring) round the odd man out.

References

Story - *Animal Seasons, Animal Homes,* Brian Wildsmith (OUP).
Rhyme - 'The big ship sails through the Alley-Alley-O' *(This Little Puffin).*
Song - The Animal Fair', *(Okki-tokki unga,* A & C Black).

B

Story - *The Blue Balloon,* by Mick Inkpen (Hodder & Stoughton).
Rhyme - 'Betty Botter' *(Puffin Book of Nursery Rhymes).*
Song - 'Ten Green Bottles', traditional.

C

Story - *The Hungry Caterpillar,* by Eric Carle (Picture Puffin).
Rhyme - 'Cats sleep anywhere', by Eleanor Farjeon *(Young Puffin Book of Verse).*
Song - 'In a Cottage in a Wood', *(Okki-tokki unga,* A & C Black).

D

Story - *Doctor Dog,* by John Talbot (Simon & Schuster Young Books).
Rhyme - 'Five little ducks went out to play' *(This Little Puffin).*
Song - 'When a dinosaur's feeling hungry', *(Game Songs with Prof. Dogg's Troupe,* A & C Black).

E

Story - *Elmer* stories, by David McKee (Red Fox Picture Book).
Rhyme - 'One grey elephant' *(This Little Puffin).*
Song - 'The Elephant' *(Appuskidu,* A & C Black)

F

Story - *Frances* stories, by Russell Hoban (Hippo Books).
Rhyme - 'One, two, three, four, five, once I caught a fish alive'.
Song - 'Five speckled frogs' *(Appuskidu,* A & C Black).

G

Story - *Mr. Gumpy* stories, by John Burningham (Jonathan Cape).
Rhyme - 'Goosey, goosey gander' *(Puffin Book of Nursery Rhymes,* Iona and Peter Opie).
Song - 'Gallop quickly', the Song of the Delhi Tongawallah *(Appuskidu,* A & C Black).

H

Story - *The happy hedgehog band,* by Martin Waddell (Walker Books).

Rhyme - 'Humpty Dumpty' and 'Hickory dickory dock'.
Song - 'The Hippopotamus Song' *(Apusskidu,* A & C Black).

I

Story - *Imagine* by Alison Lester (Viking/Puffin).
Rhyme - 'Incy Wincy Spider'.
Song - 'If you're happy and you know it' *(Everyday Singaway,* Piccolo).

J

Story - *Just like Jasper!* by Nick Butterworth and Mick Inkpen (Hodder & Stoughton).
Rhyme - 'Jack and Jill' and 'Jack be nimble'.
Song - 'Jim along Josie', *(High Low Dolly Pepper,* A & C Black).

K

Story - *Kipper,* by Mick Inkpen (Hodder & Stoughton).
Rhyme - 'Old King Cole'.
Song - 'Katie Kangaroo' *(Apusskidu,* A & C Black).

L

Story - *The bad tempered ladybird,* by Eric Carl (Hamish Hamilton)
Rhyme - 'Ladybird, ladybird'.
Song - 'Looby-loo' *(Okki-tokki unga,* A & C Black).

M

Story - *Meg and Mog* stories, by Helen Nicoll and Jan Pienkowski (Heinemann).
Rhyme - 'Mousie, mousie' *(This Little Puffin).*
Song - 'If you want to be a monster' *(Professor Dogg,* A & C Black).

N

Story - *Noisy Nora,* by Rosemary Wells (Picture Lion).
Rhyme - 'I had a little nut tree'.
Song - 'Noah' *(High Low Dolly Pepper,* A & C Black).

O

Story - *Oscar Got the Blame,* by Tony Ross (Oliver & Boyd).
Rhyme - 'Oranges and lemons'.
Song - 'Okki-tokki unga *(Okki-tokki unga,* A & C Black).

P

Story - *Three Little Pigs,* traditional.
Rhyme - 'Peter Piper', 'Pease Porridge' and 'Polly put the kettle on'.
Song - 'Punchinello', traditional.

Q
Story - *The Baked Bean Queen,* by Rose Impey and Sue Porter (Picture Puffin).
Rhyme - 'The Queen of Hearts' and 'Five little ducks'.
Song - 'Pussy cat, pussy cat', traditional.

R
Story - *Little Red Riding Hood,* traditional.
Rhyme - 'Rain, rain, go away' and 'Row, row, row your boat'.
Song - 'Sing a Rainbow', (*Apusskidu,* A & C Black).

S
Story - *The Very Busy Spider,* by Eric Carle (Hamish Hamilton).
Rhyme - 'Sing a song of sixpence' and 'Simple Simon'.
Song - 'Seagull, seagull, sit on the shore' (*This Little Puffin).*

T
Story - *Titch* stories, by Pat Hutchins (The Bodley Head).
Rhyme - 'Little Tommy Tucker' and 'Tom, Tom, the Piper's Son'.
Song - 'Tiger, tiger' (*Apusskidu,* A & C Black).

U
Story - *The Ugly Duckling,* by Hans Christian Andersen.
Song - 'Tumaluma' (*Harlequin,* A & C Black).

V
Story - *The Old Woman who lived in a Vinegar Bottle,* traditional.
Rhyme - 'Roses are red, violets are blue', traditional.

W
Story - *Mr. Wolf's Week,* by Colin Hawkins (Picture Lion).
Rhyme - 'Wee Willie Winkie'.
Song -'There was an old witch' (*Apusskidu,* A & C Black).

X
Story - *Fox in Socks,* by Dr. Seuss (Collins).
Rhyme - 'Mix a pancake' (*This Little Puffin).*

Y
Story - *Yuk Soup,* by Joy Cowley (Sunshine Books, Heinemann).
Rhyme - 'Yellow butter' *(This Little Puffin).*
Song - 'Yellow Submarine' (*Apusskidu,* A & C Black).

Z
Story - *Zug the Bug,* by Collin & Jacqui Hawkins (Picture Puffin).
Rhyme - 'Fuzzy wuzzy was a bear'.
Song - 'Going to the zoo', by Tom Paxton (*Everyday Singaway,* Piccolo).

Language Master and relevant kits (mentioned on page 10) are available from:
Drake Educational Associates, St. Fagans Road, Fairwater, Cardiff, CF5 3AE, Wales.

RECIPES

Flour Paint
I cup of flour mixed with 2 $\frac{1}{2}$ cups of water, 4 tablespoons sugar and 2 tablesoons salt. Cook in a saucepan, stirring until the mixture thickens. Cool. Mix in liquid or powder paint and adjust thickness by adding water. Spread onto paper using plastic paste spreaders.

Jammy Circles
I25g caster sugar
I00g margarine
I egg yolk
Grated rind of a lemon
200g plain flour
Water
I. Cream margarine and sugar.
2. Add egg yolk and lemon rind. Beat well.
3. Stir in flour and enough water (if necessary) to make a firm dough. (Be careful not to make dough too sticky.)
4. Roll out and cut into 6cm rounds. Cut out the centre of one half of the circles to make hoop shapes.
5. Bake at 350oF/l80oC/Gas Mark 4 - for about I5 minutes. Sandwich together with the jam.

For details of further Belair publications
please write to:

BELAIR PUBLICATIONS LTD
P.O. Box 12 TWICKENHAM TW1 2QD
England

For sales and distribution (outside USA and Canada):
Folens Publishers, Albert House, Apex Business Centre,
Boscombe Road, Dunstable, Beds. LU5 4RL, England.

For sales and distribution in USA and Canada:
Belair Publications USA, ll6 Corporation Way, Venice, Florida, 34292.